PARTICULAR SCANDALS

The Poiema Poetry Series

Poems are windows into worlds; windows into beauty, goodness, and truth; windows into understandings that won't twist themselves into tidy dogmatic statements; windows into experiences. We can do more than merely peer into such windows; with a little effort we can fling open the casements, and leap over the sills into the heart of these worlds. We are also led into familiar places of hurt, confusion, and disappointment, but we arrive in the poet's company. Poetry is a partnership between poet and reader, seeking together to gain something of value—to get at something important.

Ephesians 2:10 says, "We are God's workmanship . . ." *poiema* in Greek—the thing that has been made, the masterpiece, the poem. The Poiema Poetry Series presents the work of gifted poets who take Christian faith seriously, and demonstrate in whose image we have been made through their creativity and craftsmanship.

These poets are recent participants in the ancient tradition of David, Asaph, Isaiah, and John the Revelator. The thread can be followed through the centuries—through the diverse poetic visions of Dante, Bernard of Clairvaux, Donne, Herbert, Milton, Hopkins, Eliot, R.S. Thomas, and Denise Levertov—down to the poet whose work is in your hand. With the selection of this volume you are entering this enduring tradition, and as a reader contributing to it.

—D.S. Martin
Series Editor

Collections in this series include:
Six Sundays toward a Seventh by Sydney Lea
Epitaphs for the Journey by Paul Mariani
Within This Tree of Bones by Robert Siegel
Particular Scandals by Julie L. Moore
A Word In My Mouth by Robert Cording (*forthcoming*)
Gold by Barbara Crooker (*forthcoming*)

Particular Scandals

A Book of Poems

JULIE L. MOORE

CASCADE *Books* · Eugene, Oregon

PARTICULAR SCANDALS

Cascade Books
An Imprint of Wipf and Stock Publishers
199 W. 8th Ave., Suite 3
Eugene, OR 97401

www.wipfandstock.com

ISBN 13: 978-1-62032-788-3

Cataloging-in-Publication data:

    Moore, Julie L.

    Particular scandals / Julie L. Moore.

    xii + 84 p.; 23 cm

    ISBN 13: 978-1-62032-788-3

    1. American poetry—21st century. I. Title. II. Series.

PS3563 .O6215 P35 2013

Manufactured in the USA

Acknowledgments for *Particular Scandals*

I am grateful to the following presses for naming *Particular Scandals* (under the former title, *Scandal of Particularity*) a finalist or semi-finalist in their national book contests: The 2012 Crab Orchard Series for Poetry Open Competition (semi-finalist), The 2011 FutureCycle Poetry Press Book Award (finalist), and The 2011 Perugia Press Poetry Prize (semi-finalist).

I am also grateful to the following journals, which published my poetry, sometimes in slightly different forms or under different titles.

Alaska Quarterly Review: "Lump"
American Poetry Journal: "Clifton Gorge"
Apple Valley Review: "Buck" & "Evolution"
Assisi: An Online Journal of Arts & Letters: "One December Evening"
Atlanta Review: "Remember Blessing"
Avocet: "White-breasted Nuthatch" (reprint)
Basilica Review: "Killdeer" (under the previous title "Of Grief and Gift")
Blue Earth Review: "First Frost" & "Hells Angels"
Breakwater Review: "Blue"
Briar Cliff Review: "Will you let me write about my love for my child"
CALYX: "Intersection" (reprint)
Canary: "Hells Angels" (reprint)
Chautauqua Literary Journal: "Chicory"
Cimarron Review: "A Clear Path"
Cider Press Review: "Dark Birds"
Cherry Blossom Review: "Cherry Blossoms"
The Christian Century: "Labor Day," "Prodigal" "What We Heard on
      Christmas Day," & "Where the Rain Clears"
Coe Review: "Cicada Shells"
Comstock Review: "Shadow of Death"
Conte: A Journal of Narrative Writing: "The Grass Grows Ordinary"
Creekwalker: "Planting a Tree" (reprint)
The Cresset: "Wonder"
Dogwood: A Journal of Poetry & Prose: "Ancient Ritual" & "Harnessing
      Infinity"

Acknowledgments for Particular Scandals

The Fairfield Review: "White-breasted Nuthatch"
Flint Hills Review: "Does soil hurt"
Flyway: Journal of Writing and Environment: "Ohio"
The Fourth River: "Something to Amaze" & "Stealth"
Green Hills Literary Lantern: "Window"
Journal of Truth and Consequence: "Abundance," "Family Portrait," &
    "Sightseeing"
Literature and Belief: "Arioso on Wings"
Mad Poets Review: "Buck" (reprint)
The Missouri Review Online: "Recovery"
New Madrid: "Amen and Amen" & "Waiting Room"
Orion Headless: "Pessimist"
Pirene's Fountain: "The Painted Lady and the Thistle"
Poemeleon: A Journal of Poetry: "Particular Scandals"; "Amen and Amen"
    & "Harnessing Infinity" (reprints)
Poetry Friends: "Royal Candles" & "Planting a Tree" (reprints)
Redux: "Ancient Ritual" (reprint)
Relief: A Quarterly Christian Expression: "Arrival" (under the previous title
    "Of Apples and Amnesia") & "Prayer Shawl"
Riverwind: "Intersection"
Rock & Sling: "Peace Lily"
Ruminate: "Confession," "Kyrie Eleison," "The first time I saw a shooting
    star," & "Planting a Tree"
Schuylkill Valley Journal: "Return"
Sou'Wester: "Denouement" & "I Have Something to Say"
Switched-on Gutenberg: "Voice" (reprint)
Terrain.org: "Does soil hurt" (reprint)
A Time of Singing: "Eating Her Way through December" & "Wonder"
    (reprint)
Two Review: "Opening Day"
Valparaiso Poetry Review: "Afterlife"
Willow Review: "Royal Candles" & "Voice"
Your Daily Poem: "Clifton Gorge," "Killdeer," & "I Have Something to Say"
    (reprints)

Likewise, I thank the publications below that have honored my poetry in the following ways.

- "Afterlife," "Blue," "The Grass Grows Ordinary," and "Killdeer" were included in a group of poems that received an International Merit Award from the *Atlanta Review* in its 2012 international poetry contest.

- "The Painted Lady and the Thistle" was the Web Weekly Feature on *Verse Daily* the week of May 2, 2011 and was nominated for inclusion in Sundress Publications' 2011 *Best of the Net* anthology.

- "Recovery" was featured as The Poem of the Week on *The Missouri Review Online* and received honorable mention in the 2010 poetry contest sponsored by Writecorner Press.

- "Stealth" was named a runner-up in the 2009 poetry contest sponsored by *The Fourth River*.

- "Harnessing Infinity" was a finalist for the 2009 *Dogwood* Poetry Prize.

- "Confession" won the Janet B. McCabe Poetry Prize from *Ruminate* magazine in 2008.

- A group of five poems, four of which appear in *Particular Scandals*— "Ancient Ritual," "I Have Something to Say," "Remember Blessing," and "Shadow of Death"—was a finalist in the 2007 *Many Mountains Moving* Poetry Contest.

- "White-breasted Nuthatch" was named an Editor's Choice in the fall 2006 issue of *The Fairfield Review*.

In addition, I am grateful to the following presses for including my poems in their anthologies:

- University of Nebraska–Lincoln Gender Programs for including "Recovery" in *Becoming: What Makes a Woman* (2012)

- *Magnapoets* for including "The first time I saw a shooting star" and "Window" in its anthology entitled, *Many Windows* (2011)

- Outrider Press for including "Chicory" in *Seasons of Change* (2010)

- City Works Press for including "Lump" in *Mamas and Papas* (2010)

Acknowledgments for Particular Scandals

I thank the wonderful poets, Barbara Crooker, Lynnell Edwards, Maureen Fry, Jeff Gundy, and Jeanne Murray Walker for their insightful comments about my poems that led to many successful revisions. I'm also deeply grateful to Sally Rosen Kindred for the time she took with my manuscript and for her thoroughness in suggesting a sensible and aesthetically pleasing structure for the book. Likewise, I'm appreciative of the Antioch Writers' Workshop (AWW), where I was a work fellow in 2008 and which awarded me the Judson Jerome Poetry Scholarship in 2009. The feedback I gained from my fellow poets there as well as my workshop leaders, John Drury and Ed Davis, and AWW-manuscript consultant, Rebecca McClanahan, was likewise invaluable. My thanks to Cedarville University as well for release time to work on this book.

Finally, I am grateful to my beloved husband John, who walked these paths of joy and suffering with me, and our children, Ashley and Alex, who at young ages encountered both God and pain and inspire me by how they consistently choose faith and love over despair and bitterness.

Table of Contents

Table of Contents

three

To John, Ashley, & Alex

If we had a keen vision and feeling of all ordinary human life, it would be like hearing the grass grow or the squirrel's heartbeat, and we should die of the roar which lies on the other side of silence.

    −GEORGE ELIOT, *MIDDLEMARCH*

All things of grace and beauty such that one holds them to one's heart have a common provenance in pain. Their birth in grief and ashes.

    −CORMAC McCARTHY, *THE ROAD*

That Christ's incarnation occurred improbably, ridiculously, at such-and-such a time, into such-and-such a place, is referred to . . . as "the scandal of particularity." Well the "scandal of particularity" is the only world that I, in particular, know. . . . We're all up to our necks in this particular scandal. . . . I never saw a tree that was no tree in particular; I never met a man, not the greatest theologian, who filled infinity, or even whose hand, say, was undifferentiated, fingerless, like a griddle cake, and not lobed and split just so with the incursions of time.

    −ANNIE DILLARD, *PILGRIM AT TINKER CREEK*

one

Amen and Amen

I'm sitting on my front porch
    by an open window. The breeze,
        tinged with the copper of coins,
will purchase rain by morning.

Inside, my daughter's playing the piano,
    singing Cohen's *Hallelujah*,
        her voice rising, the keys
stirring sparrows in pine trees and maples.

I want to care about her music,

but I'm reading O'Connor, considering *displaced*
    persons, the ungodly ways we ruin one another.
        Banks have ruptured like arteries
while CEOs drink Bloody Marys.

Broke, a man kills himself in Chicago.
    On the page, the priest mentions Jesus.
        Mrs. McIntyre snaps, says Jesus doesn't belong,
damns his name. Their words

blaze like Ashley's song, like the light

glowing at our front door, drawing a moth.
    Night descends around me like a net.
        The monarchs have long since left
for Mexico. They're getting drunk on cheap

nectar and spawning larvae that slurp
    the toxic juice of milkweed.
        Their cells pack on poison like muscles.
When they burst from their chrysalises,

their wings sprout orange—loud
    and clear—proclaiming
        to every hungry predator
how terrible they taste. Hallelujah.

And other butterflies are question marks.

The pearly punctuation etched
    like a hieroglyph on their hindwings.
        Their curvaceous edges
silhouettes of every explanation we seek.

Pain is my appendage again.

(Surely, I've done this before). Sutures
    from my sixth surgery sting.
        Within the house,
my husband calls the dog, her tags

jangling like the crickets.
    Ashley sings on, as though her breath's
        no longer her own, absorbed now
in benediction. Our amen un-

broken, like a world without end.

Confession

Mark 5:24–34

And in the twelfth year, there was still
        blood. And so many difficult degrees

of separation. Everything, at this point,
        burned. The once-soft skin of her labia.

The pathetic pulp of her womb.
        And the mass of hard questions.

Pressing on her like the crowds
        bearing down on him.

She knew the rules: Keep your hands
        to yourself. Whatever you touch you foul.

But she reached for him anyway.
        Fastened her un-

clean fingers, tipped
        with outrageous nerve,

onto the lip of his cloak.
        While he sensed the tug

of the siphon, the precious liquid of his power
        tapped, she felt her river of red

drain, the fierce spear of her pain
        withdraw.

He wanted to know who grasped
      such scandalous and particular

faith. Never again would she soil
      a place where she lay. So she fell

at his feet. Confessed.

Shadow of Death

You can't forget the grave
once you've stared down its well
of despair, pondering its promise

of reprieve, a permanent stay of pain's stubborn
execution. I wish I would, of course.
I wish I would not see myself

in silhouettes drawn by the dark lines
of disease, in figures like Roth's
Millicent Kramer who swallowed

all her pills to extinguish the flames
of affliction, to leave Everyman
to join everyone who'd gone before her.

I wish I would see myself
only in the resurrected versions,
like impatiens, choked by a string

of rainless days, breaking free,
unfurling their pink tongues
beneath the burst of silver clouds,

or that man in the news who awoke—
Praise the Lord!—cancerless,
yawning and stretching while the grim reaper

looked the other way. Oh, I know
I'm like them, like Lazarus who rose
to the challenge of a new life. But I can't seem

to cut off the shadow
of that death. No, it stays with me,
nipping at my heels,

following me wherever I go.

Evolution

I have so many scars,
    I gave up on vitamin E long ago,
        I tell my daughter after my laparoscopy.

She suggested we could bond
    by applying the greasy ointment to our skin
        together—her to her knee, dislocated

last summer, her surgery leaving
    a purple, worm-like scar,
        and me to the three hyphens on my abdomen.

But I've had many operations—
    I feel like the Titanic
        sinking while the crew throws things

overboard—appendix, ovary, gall bladder—
    organ after organ tossed into the sea
        of my mortality. Sometimes, I imagine

they adapt to their new surroundings,
    sprouting fins, morphing vessels into gills,
        swimming onto shore. And I wonder

if they'll meet me there someday
    along with heart and mind and soul,
        having formed by then, hands for me to hold.

You're laughing, I bet, at the notion of fins
    on an ovary, gills on the gall bladder,
        and those preposterous hands. But admit it:

You'd like something or someone to meet you there, too,
    pull you up from the sand in that strange
        and solitary land. For you sense

your new appendage, though entirely
        unexpected—is it evolving even now?—
            might be fear.

Killdeer

If I defer the grief I will diminish the gift. —Eavan Boland

1.

My parents care what happens
to the killdeer whose nest of eggs
rests in their lawn. They worry

about the family in the storms that come.
The four inches of rain that falls in one night,
flooding the roads, the creeks, their yard.

My dad wants to harness the silver-
shingled cover of clouds, the warmth
in their electric touch, the very water.

To keep the mother alive whose cries overflow
the banks of her throat. To defend her unborn
chicks growing cold from exposure.

2.

Beaks poke through,
rip in two the mottled fabric of the eggs.

Emerge. Tender and tentative,
like buds that one morning decide, finally,

to rise from their bed, get dressed.
And then: the fluffing of feathers, the flurry

of squeals. Like kids at a birthday bash, cheering
as the piñata breaks open, spills

sweets. Life is like that.
It tends to celebrate itself.

And my parents run outside to witness
the chicks' first steps, finding irresistible

the urge to crash the party.

Prayer Shawl

Knit like the vertebrae in his spine
    before he broke it
when he hanged himself years ago,
    the shawl his mother made
wraps around me as I pray.
    I kneel, pain from last night's
sex, fifty pins embedded
    in the tender cushion
of my vulva. Love, I have discovered,
    cannot heal some wounds.
Threads of arthritis entwine
    her knees. She cannot genuflect.
And her husband is dead,
    two of her four sons, dead—
all in the same year.
    But that one survived.
A new man now, he sits with her
    every day, the two of them
wielding their needles,
    fashioning shawl after need-
thick shawl, praying
    for those, like me,
to once again be whole.

Recovery

Walking along my front porch, I rub my swollen
    belly like I did, years ago, when I was expecting

a miracle. I am empty, gutted
    like the old farmhouse across the street,

every room pared down to the frame's
    bare bones. Even the floors have been removed.

All I want is a day when the pain
    breaks. I've had seven surgeries now—

adhesions excised like splinters,
    four rundown organs

pulled out like windows and walls.
    Here in mid-life, I'm nothing but pure

ruin. And part of me would like to give up,
    dissolve into dust like my neighbor's brick.

But in the ash trees that line our road,
    in flawless iambs, the sparrows chant

preserve, preserve, preserve, preserve.
    And I step into our yard where bees,

persistent as repeated pleas,
    poise themselves before the roses,

then bury their faces in the velvet
    breasts, suckling sugar, tasting

grace as insistent as the tune they hum.

Denouement

One vulture sits on a fence post,
another atop a telephone pole that sways
as it throws its big-breasted body around.
They scattered to these perches when I opened
the door, knowing the squeak
would pry
         them from the neighbor's cat,
stiff on the road, one eye bulging.

But my daughter is glad they're here
to clean up, eat that eye.
She wants it gone.

So I go back in, close the door.

The fence sitter hops
         down,
walks to the body. And the phone fowl
swoops in.

Now we have drama.

Fanning its great wings, the early bird,
like a godfather, chases off its unwelcome cousin.
Claims the territory, circumambulating
the fresh meat. The relative
now distant,
         a wing span away.
The boss picks at a paw, lifts it up.
Then beaks the butt, pulls
         the sinews like taffy.

A third party flies through birch branches,
breaking off twigs, sending orange leaves fluttering
to the ground. It lands.
                              Wants in.

Now two wait, one on each side,
like body guards, their stomachs urging
mutiny, their impulse stamped down
like the don's feet on the fur.

Not now, not now, not now.

When a car comes, they all take flight,
circling the goods, scheming for a new angle.
But they return under the same chain
of command. And this will go on all day,
flesh, like the hours,
                              unraveling
till dusk.

Harnessing Infinity

My daughter wants me to harness infinity.
Her algebra teacher taught her formulas,
four in all,
                for bridling the immeasurable like horses.
I know why she wants me to do it.
She needs me to take her father's heart
in my hands, heal it like Jesus
moved muscles so tongues could flex,
eyes could lift, and legs could stretch.
But I don't have the power of God.
And the numbers in the math are
imaginary.
                I sense the black mustang,
wild with will, the wind like a whip at its back,
approaching.
                All I can do is gather
alfalfa in the fields, pour countless oats
into the pail. Ease the sting
of thirst in its throat with water
pulled from my well.

First Frost

Killdeer squealing in flight above the fields—
chill hanging on the air like breath—
water dangling from rain spouts, dripping
residue of night onto the deck—
burning bushes below not yet ablaze,
silent as matches unstruck—
white ice in the shadows of houses and clouds
lingering like dust—

And I'm thinking of how leaves unhinge
from the ash trees and settle on their spines.
How the beloved, home from the hospital,
heart healing, simply sneezes inside.
How death will come calling one inevitable dawn
like this killdeer now landing on our glittering lawn.

Dark Birds

The season has taken a stab
    at despondency. Note the nickel-plated sky,

its stony countenance. And the sallow grass,
    how stunted its stature has become.

And all these dark birds: Starlings swarming,
    swirling like a tornado that keeps touching

down. Crows crowding the fields,
    feeding on nothing but crumbs

of cornstalks. The mourning dove, balancing
    its solo act on a telephone wire, crooning

its Irish tune of lonesomeness and longing.
    Looks like despair to me.

Except for those red-winged blackbirds
    flaunting their epaulets atop cattails.

Do you see them rise, then ride the back
    of the wind, scattering their staccato notes

like seeds along the way?
    They, too, witnessed the first dropped

leaf, perceived how green withdrew
    its lovely face from the landscape.

So how do they do it, lifting their own
    hearts as they soar toward the clouds?

Don't they ever, like the rest of us,
    tire of transcending?

Family Portrait

I'll be dead in two weeks
you said after we posed for the photograph
in our twenty-first year together.

It was good we did it, you said,
so the kids and I could look at you in your last days
for the rest of our lives.

You'd found your third clot in your leg,
the bruise behind your knee
spreading like a crooked smile.

Your blood pressed hard
against your arteries, lashing out
like an ungrateful child.

Your heart you feared wicked,
the thing that failed you once
and despite all the promises,

might fail you again soon.
O how grief has hung on us,
nailed to our home like an image on a wall.

Our heads pounding with the memory
of death's unforgettable face,
a face that was here and there

and everywhere, conspicuous
in the picture of your health.

The first time I saw a shooting star,

I was 42, and the world was busy casting
its orange shadow onto the surface of the moon.

The red eye of a plane was blinking
as it slipped beneath Orion's belt,

the rumble of the engine too far away to hear.

Icicles, invisible in the dark,
crackled in the near-zero air,

splitting their grips,
tinkling like glass as tips reached

the sleet-topped snow below.

The wind was still, asleep in its cloudless bed.
The wafer of wonder, crisp on my tongue.

My prayer, simple,
spoken aloud like the soft call of an owl:

O God, maker of heaven and earth, heal my husband.

Then the flame, light years old,
streamed through the sky.

And I was as skeptical as you are now,
my faith in any true goodness

eclipsed by the pain in my life.

But I tell you, it happened like this:
visible as the disappearing moon,

the light, long-awaited, arrived.

Something to Amaze

There is one advantage
in not knowing everything,
in walking through fields
time and time again, still finding
something to amaze—
like these three birches
huddling together, feet
wedged in ice, snow
sifting through their arms.
And the shiver in those arms.
Their silent torsos
thick with acquiescence.

Peace Lily

I waited all year for the return of splendor,
the resurrection of the spathiphyllum given to us
when the lining in my husband's artery
peeled back, then flapped like a flag,
clogging his flow of blood.

I doused it daily, trying to follow
the directions to keep the soil moist.
So the dying began.
And it didn't take long, though I changed
the way I watered.

Leaf after leaf wilted, each edge
singeing, then curling under,
wrapping its once open palm
into a limp fist.
The condition seemed irreversible.

Only three leaves on one stalk survived.
By Christmas, my kids said the plant looked
like Charlie Brown's pathetic tree.
Offered ornaments. Suggested tinsel and lights.
My husband's blood pressure rose

as the lily drooped.
He joked it was bad luck, or a bad omen,
said we should throw it out,
the whole thing was hopeless.
But I held onto it like a charm.

And I fed its roots through the winter,
watched it sprout one, then two leaves.
Nursed it in April, May, and June
as its foliage fanned out. Even talked to it
in the summer, cajoling it to grow

tall as Ohio corn. And the white blossom,
beautiful as the peace in its name,
impressive as my husband's now-whole heart,
unbelievable as God's honest truth,
unfurled its autumn blessing.

Particular Scandals

1.

A newlywed drives his bride to her death,
sliding on ice, slamming the passenger door
into an oncoming car. By, as they say,
accident.
                    An only child is crushed,
the walls of his school
falling on his head. And hundreds
more like him. Killed,
as insurance records note,
by an act of God.

How we struggle with the particular face
of suffering.
                    The avalanche
in the young father's artery.
The undertow of pain, pulling,
not letting go of the wife
and mother. The slow drip
of cancer in the preschooler.
The young girl shackled to the shrine
of man's need. A girl I do not know.
A daughter who is every daughter in the world.

2.

There are infinite ways
to suffer. I've missed one.
Of course I have.
Or a million.

Let me not
count the ways.

3.

Why not disavow God, and say, once
and for all, he does not exist,
or if he does, he is not good?

4.

Yet.

5.

Think: Tomorrow morning when I rise
with the sun to start another day,

will I notice the particular
drops of dew glistening like stars?

Will I fall to my knees, see
the blades of grass sucking in

light like breath?

Will I hear the mist whispering
to the pines or follow the swallow

to her nest, watch her drop beetles
into the tiny beaks, hear the silence

of satisfaction that follows?
Will I feel the warmth of her wings

as they cover her chicks' downy heads?

6.

It depends, I suppose,
on what I'll need that morning.
If my tea is hot, my juice sweet,
the jam on my toast tart,
if the paper is full of the same ruin
that happens every day, if I feel self-
sufficient, smart, even a tad proud,
if I'm in a hurry, maybe even late,
if I'm still half asleep,
if this same wretched headache lingers,
if I just have things to do,
it might slip

7.

past my attention, unnoticed
like a shy idea that stands mute
against the wall of the mind,
finding it difficult to express itself
out loud.

8.

Oh, the other side
of silence.

That death-inducing
roar.

9.

Blame is an easier game.

10.

Hyacinth and huckleberry.
Hopkins' beloved bluebell.
Deepening. Blooming.
Like the intelligent

design of a newborn's lungs.
Isn't it scandalous, I wonder, to praise
nothing
for creating beauty

as particular as these?

two

The Painted Lady and the Thistle

The painted lady alights on thistle,
    its winged mosaic aflutter with brilliance

and thirst. Here is Adam again,
    his brow stitched in toil,
his back breaking out in sweat.

    What will the blossom, edged
with thorny predicaments, offer

    as this butterfly plunges
its proboscis into the core
    ablaze with being?

Of course you already know.
    Every sip, a miracle, a curse

that never disappoints the one
    whose instinct is to drink
first, ask questions later.

Arrival

We feel it in the air: the chill
of change. Even the blue deepens
like the world's flipped over,

and the ocean's filled the sky.

Which means November will soon rain
down, and the death
of everything is inevitable.

The trees will let fly
their golden leaves.
All will go brown and barren.

And cold.

It'll feel like God has left us
as only the wind fills
the silence. We'll feel like hiding.

We'll forget the glory days:
pools of sun, embrace of earth, show
of skin. We'll even forget that apples

arrive in the fall.

Abundance

My neighbor's orchard looks like Christmas,
red and green apples like glass balls
brimming on branches,

though the sweet flesh is so heavy,
some stems snap.

Fallen, the fruit will fill
with songs of worms.

The grove smells like blue
cradling the October sky, like the end
of hunger, like grace in the tender

dance of sacrifice, one life for another,
the skin soon to be pierced

with blade, or thorn-
sharp bite.

Christmas Stillborn

'Tis the season
of death—

ground entombed in ice,
shrubs embalmed,

trees mere bones
creaking in north winds—

and everything pales
in its face—

clouds anemic, grass
listless, air ashen.

In such, you bury
your son so long expected.

Where are wonder and miracle
in the collage of his cries?

We wonder at the grave
of our anticipation.

What We Heard on Christmas Day

with a line from Longfellow

Silence like early morning, like indigo
deepening at the bottom of the sea.
For hundreds of years.

No voice to say *this is the way*.
Or *tomorrow, he comes*. They raised
their questions, rose each morning, found

no answers. Unless you count
Wait. But after the hush
of prophecy, the long line of law,

exile centuries ago just a bitter aftertaste
in their empty mouths, sting
of dust on their ribs dulled, almost imperceptible,

a baby wailed. And if you listened close,
you knew your ears did not deceive you.
He had entered the ebony tomb

of Earth, loosening at last his long-held tongue,
the star a halo of song blaring overhead,
God is not dead, nor doth He sleep.

Wonder

Amazing love! How can it be? —Charles Wesley

How did you do it?
Your disappearance
from glory, your break
into humanity?
                    Did you let the Father
scoop splendor from you
till you were hollowed
like heaven when you left?

How did the scraping go?
And how much did it hurt?
                            Or did the Spirit put you
under, tell you when you'd awake
you'd be good as new,
like the silk-spun skin
of a baby born that day?
No pain because you wouldn't know,
not yet, what you'd let go?
                        How did eternity
squeeze itself into the folds
of fat in your thighs,
how did all that light
funnel itself into your bones,
how did your breath, this time,
fill your own lungs?
                    And how
did your open hands
furl into tiny fists,
fists you'd never shake at the skies?

Universe

Did you know that if you stand in your yard
just after dusk

lifting your eyes like a prayer
to the heavens

& peer into snow falling
toward you,

your senses will swirl
& you can pretend, well enough,

that you are in another
world—you & the weightless

pearls dropping
from the sky's broken neck-

lace—& you will spin
in orbit somewhere else

anywhere but here
in the universe of pain?

Pessimist

Just when your resolve was thawing
like the late winter ground,
the freezing fists of rain

beat on your door, insisting
you let the icy body of gloom back in.
You must survive the pain of impending

loss. You can't go soft now.
You can't stand at your window, watching blackbirds
gather amid the old snow on the only patch of grass

exposed, foraging for something
to sustain themselves. You might be amazed
by what they find on that green space.

By what, after being buried like the dead,
would still feed them. You must brace yourself,
fearing even hope is a storm you must weather.

White-breasted Nuthatch

I'm into ornithology now—
it's poetry's fault the birds

zoom into this line
or that, and I don't want to say,

generically, *bird*—no anonymous
fowls for me, no!—I want to write

Yellow-rumped Warbler or *Scarlet Tanager*
or here, this one, *White-breasted Nuthatch.*

Ah, yes, this one can skip along the trunk of a tree
like a stone across a pond. And it can hammer

at seeds and peck for bugs while its hind nail
digs into bark, balancing

its plush body on the primal edge
of wonder.

Opening Day

with two lines from Hemingway

April showers surged as the temperature slipped
    down its red slide into the cold
        pool of dawn. And the creek roiled
        as it filled and overspilled

its banks. Then thunder
    spoke words of snow
        surreal as paradox,
          as the sight of beauty

just before death,
    petals of the white rose
        filleting the loin of air
          as they fall to the ground.

I stood on my deck, amazed,
    watched flakes fluttering
        and an old man standing in the wild
        stream as it lunged

through his legs. He kept plunging
    his hands into the dark waters,
        grasping at something
          elusive, like a shadow, or a dream,

snatching nothing but a cramp.
    So he shook his left hand with zeal,
        as if to unhook
          a leech embedded in his muscle.

And he talked to himself aloud, hailing
    Mary, then wondering,
        What would the great DiMaggio do?
           like he was looking for inspiration.

Then he turned,
    craned his neck,
        cast his body so it arced
           like a fishing line

over the water, and with him,
    my eyes strained to catch
        the great erect tail
           slicing through the dark.

Cherry Blossoms

Weightless as a pink swab
of cotton candy, each blossom

clings to the sapling's branches,
altogether,

heavy as awe
overpowering the senses.

So the limbs
sag. And the tree

hunches from the burden
of bloom it carries,

that bundle of beauty
it soon will drop.

I Have Something to Say

Indulge me.
    Let me tell you how today, filled
        with fancy, she fell to her face,
perfuming herself

with eau de earth, eau de clover,
    eau de grasshopper, worm, beetle,
        romping in the grass, in the salubrious air
thick with spring and all things new.

And scattered throughout our adjoining acre,
    a thousand dandelions,
        the heads of old men nodding,
hardly hanging on to their white hair.

She wanted to go there, roll in that field, too,
    release all those seeds into the atmosphere—
        kick up a sweet and wild bouquet
and her own gleeful sneezing

as they'd float like feathers in the breeze,
    land like snowflakes on her black coat.
        O, that Labrador look, that side-slung tongue,
those boisterous, brown eyes that yes, I'll just say it,

embody bliss. What luxury
    here on the green lap
        of Ohio, here and nowhere else,
I tell you today and no other day.

Ancient Ritual

In the sky, you see a dark cloud swell
        into the shape of Africa, a continent of impending

downpour. Sense taps on your ribs,
        a Morse code from your mind to move you

in the right direction. Then memory kicks in,
        that hopeless romantic who insists

some encounters happen in ways
        you're old enough to know can't be true.

But you're eight again anyway,
        and your mother shouts from the house as the thunder

rumbles overhead. You stand like a sycamore,
        scabbed and scarred from moments like this,

ignoring your orders in your own backyard, an absence
        without leave beneath the spellbinding spray.

And the tribe of silver drops
        drums on your tongue as you offer your empty self

like a cup to the Lord of the storm.
        Your bare feet disappear

in the fast-forming puddles
        while the wind cuts loose

a lithe length of willow. You raise it up,
        wave your hands, jump, circle

the tree, wild with wonder, or worship,
          or something you can't quite name,

something ancient as day and real
          as the rain now falling,

rhythmic in its familiar ritual,
          on your all-grown-up face.

Arioso on Wings

I am still confident of this: I will see the goodness of the Lord in the land of the living. —Psalm 27:13

A trumpet trills like the throat of a lily,
vibrato on a bumblebee's tongue.
While *Arioso for Brass* plays, I watch

sheep graze on the knoll,
moving clumsily along every few minutes
like leaves in a lazy breeze,

bumping into one another, head
to wool-wadded rump. Blackbirds dart
in and out of cherry trees, drinking in ruby

juice like Bach's melody imbibes smooth
intonations. Beneath morning sun,
last night's rainwater sluices

through the creek bed, an epiphany
spilling over the hillside. Nearby, the neighbor's dog
digs a hole, plunging his nose

into his earthen bowl. In the pasture, geese
splash in puddles as the cows
dip their necks to tug

on wet blades like notes on a soul.
One cranes her neck toward her flank, shoots
out her tongue to lick at a fly-

induced itch, her black fur rippling,
tail twirling. Another lows like a tuba.
And it's goodness (isn't it?) here in the land

of the living, riding on this silken air,
sliding like a trombone through the whorls
of corn, pulsing like green,

iridescent on hummingbird wings.

Clifton Gorge

There lives the dearest freshness deep down things . . .
—*Gerard Manley Hopkins*

Balsam floods the woods,
    swathing our senses
like moss swaddles roots and earth.
    Ferns flutter in the shadow
of the wind moving through,
    while we descend into the sanctuary
of the gorge like the sun lowers
    its long beams through the green
lattice of leaves above. We hope
    to hit bottom as the thrush

throws its deep voice across the ravine
    where a woodpecker knocks on a door
of oak and a lip of limestone loosens,
    tumbles down, greets us at the stream,
which even now rips through rock,
    then pools its energy along the banks
where minnows animate
    the ruin, stirring the cup
brimming with revival, their small bodies,
    flashes of hallelujah.

Royal Candles

My husband rarely brings me flowers
from stores. Instead, he plants
a rainbow of pansies, impatiens, roses,
plunging his bare hands into soil.
Sometimes, he doesn't wear shoes.
He likes the way the earth feels
as it rubs into his skin, penetrates
beneath his nails, wedding flesh

to land. This is majestic work.
This, an extravagant life. So when sun
rises like a flame, lighting the Royal
Candles he nurtures, they burn
purple, and on this noble
ground I feel like a queen.

Hells Angels

Ablaze with buzz like the motors that drone
as cycles pass by,

bumblebees, in their striped jackets,
black helmets, and snug gloves,

cruise through the coreopsis
while their pollen passengers hug them tight.

And when my water splashes the blooms,
they rev their engines and peel out—

sun soaking their necks,
wind flying in their faces—

and they guzzle like Hells Angels
the nectar of an open road.

Cicada Shells

We used to pluck them from tree trunks like berries from vines. Collect them in jars. So fragile, we could crush them with a Charmin squeeze. Which we did at times, just to hear the crackle, to feel the force of our fingers. And other targets were as easy to find. Skins of snakes we wielded like swords in our kid-sized hands, then thrashed against arms. Grasshopper corpses on the driveway we kicked like stones. And the live ones: spiders and ants we squashed under the tips of our toes. Brittle backs of beetles we crunched like bones. Pill bugs we smashed so they oozed like pus. We raised killing to an art, pillaging to the music of cicadas, their husky bellies pulsating on buttonball bark.

Return

Walking through the tall grass, our legs push against the muscle of the meadow. The weeds wild with wetness, burs sticking to our jeans like fat ticks. All is new in the blue-green morning. And aromatic as earth itself. Scent of seeds. Puff of pollen. We, like the bees, sense the field is fringed with flavor. Topped with tassels we chew on. Coffeeweed roasts in the summer sun. Brown-eyed Susans stare at us like suspicious parents. We laugh. We shout just to hear our voices bounce like balls off the Poconos' walls. Let each return like a favor. Like a promise, long forgotten, finally fulfilled. Like the hills we roll down. Till the grass, towering over us at the bottom, catches us. Wraps us in its grasp.

Ohio

Hello, Ohio / The back roads / I know Ohio / Like the back of my hand.
—Over the Rhine

My New Jersey cousin says it's boring
to run here in the rural area where I live,

past acres of corn and soybean and canola,
unyielding to variation,

landmarking nothing other than one full sweep
of green. I note each row as I go by,

listen to the prayers whispered by the leaves,
long and short,

which bow when summer heaps on heat
or rustle in praise after fresh fallen rain.

I am not the farmer who's planted the seeds
or moved among the stalks to measure

the wealth of his work or the ruins of deer.
I know that. I know I haven't really earned

what blessing this land gives.
But still, it's not boredom I feel

as I walk the dog along the road
for the umpteenth time,

sun sinking, lavender light spreading its wings,
gliding over these unflinching fields.

three

Prodigal

The farmer has shown up with the sun,
the two conspiring to work the land together.

It's time for blades to dig in,
furrow a fresh start.

And you'd like to join in. You'd like to whistle
the sun over to you like an obedient dog,

tell it to sit, right there, and stay while you seek
forgiveness. For too long, you've been trapped,

burrowing with your bare hands tunnel after dead-
end tunnel, stubborn, refusing to change

direction as you search for the yellow face
of escape to glow before your eyes, unveil

the mysterious egress. Go.
You can see it now. Turn

your hands over like the dirt at your knees,
the soil on that field. And go.

Does soil hurt

when the tulip pushes through?
You may think this question silly, say
the soil isn't human with feelings
or animal with instinct, is more like a table
that can't answer when someone knocks
for good luck, laugh when someone pulls
its leg, or scream when someone's knife
digs in. Is oblivious.

But I see a sharp tip as the bud pierces
the sepia skin like a thick needle, then red
like blood hitting air. And it inhales
like a babe who sucks in first breath,
tight-fisted, rooting for the milk of mother
earth, the throbbing womb it's just split
open. Do you know any way life comes forth
without pain?

Afterlife

This week, a foal, auburn and awkward, emerges
from the barn down the road, presses close
to the mare as they trot inside the fence,
then lies in the grass, flapping its tail like a wing.

It's all the rage of the neighborhood.

The owner raises race horses,
though he told me he bet only once in his life—
after his son-in-law died in a car crash.
He won, gave the money to his daughter.

He's been retired a long time now.

He once taught English, then became superintendent.
Before that, the Philippines, his tour where he kept MacArthur's
word. And before that, the orphanage where he met his late wife,
a childhood with nerve amid the world's first breakdown.

So this is his afterlife: Racing against beasts

and time. Every year, birthing new hope,
then tethering it to the earth. Each foal a scandal
of particular beauty, its legs, like his, surveying
the soft lay of land. The sun resting

on each shoulder like a hand.

Intersection

I never drive through this intersection
& not think of you & that day
your car skidded on ice,
then slid perpendicular

into the oncoming car.
The day your brain bruised
beyond all cure, like an apple
colliding with a concrete floor.

The day your organs, packed
in ice, were carried in coolers
across Ohio. Your eyes
to a girl born blind. Your heart

to a father amid his farewells.
Your kidneys, your liver,
your twenty-year-old skin.
How your body gave in spite of itself.

I pull through now, my son a passenger
(like you were then) who's slipping
on the interstice of adolescence,
who wants a map to follow, to detour

the impact of his unswerving despair.
I feel like your husband, the one who'll live
with wounds, who wants us to emerge
from the road unscathed

but can't control the wheel.

Voice

My friend, the mom of a beautiful
    20-year-old poet, who this month,
        on a Tuesday, silenced himself with gas,
can't understand why God took him.

For in the same moment her son began to gasp,
    across town, her daughter drove her car
        into a ditch. And God saved *her*.
As she opened her dented door,

my friend entered *his* bedroom, found his body,
    still and blue, the memory of his birth
        pushing through her, his head crowning,
lungs launching, face roaring red.

And one week later—to the day—
    his slapstick games and existential
        hair, unruly questions and acoustic guitar,
his how-to-save-a-life voice

all came rushing back
    as she checked her voice mail,
        listening, for the first time,
to a message from months ago,

surfacing from a place, which until then,
    had been nebulous and remote,
        like the space between satellites—
her one and only son saying,

Hey, mom, I arrived fine.

The Grass Grows Ordinary

It's nine o'clock and the flesh of evening turns
     pink as salmon. My husband calls me to the porch
where we sit, watching our son and his friend,
     their faces aglow with rose,

tossing their blossom-leathered ball.
     Our sidewalk blushes, the lawn dons
rouge. My grandmother died this morning
     just before my grandfather walked

through the door of the nursing home.
     When my aunt arrived, he raised
his coffee cup, said, *Hey, kid, want some?*
     The rest of the family, on the other side

of the country, was still in church.
     So my aunt left us messages,
her words, steeped in grief's briny
     distillation, greeted us as we returned

home. A neighbor's bottle rocket
     whines, shearing the dream-like
fabric of dusk, erupts in green applause,
     then falls silent as a star. Why,

my sister and I will wonder later,
     didn't Grandmom wait
till after her daily lunch with Granddad?
     What, my mom calls to ask, *will you wear*

to the funeral? A car door slams
     in the distance. The light fades in minutes.
Already, the concrete pales, the grass
     grows ordinary in its dark suit.

Lump

Of coal. In your stocking. Solid mass in the toe. Or in your throat
if you're a coal miner right before the rush of rock like rain falls
on your head. You know you're trapped. The canary's trilling long
since silenced. Or, speaking of being underground, the hill by
your drive. (The one you're tempted to make into a mountain.)
The mole's tunnel leaving the soil soft as a freshly dug grave. Step.
Sink. Feel the earth give way. The way it gave and gave and kept
on giving when the doctor said, *here, yes, here, I don't want you to
be overly concerned but right here* (in your daughter's breast—she's
fifteen) *I can feel it.*

Chicory

Chicory unfolds its petals like arms,
    blooming blue each sunrise in June.
        Looking at the fields, you could swear

the sky has capsized. The story
    goes like this: Spurned by a blossoming girl,
        some surly, red-faced god turned her

into these weeds. Every day,
    as her roots grind past noon,
        as she tries in vain to cast off

the curse, if you close your eyes,
    breathe in the tight air,
        you can sense her periwinkle

pretense. You won't be surprised
    when the world inverts,
        when afternoon sun forces

her bow, seals her in her own
    embrace, when the meadow
        clouds with Queen Anne's lace.

Waiting Room

You sit in the waiting room as the old farmer speaks
the doctor's name like any other name. Like normal.

I hear he's good, the hospital receptionist replies.
I've met him. He seems like the nicest guy.

And once again, you sit with your tongue
locked behind your teeth.

You've kept quiet for years
since she asked you to (his ex-

wife, that is), afraid as she was for her own
life. But your thoughts grow

loud as banging pots, your memory howls like a dog
eyeing an intruder. You know the real

story. How her upstanding doctor-
husband slapped her through all seven

pregnancies. How he delivered the babies
himself to hide the bruises

at home. How he punched like pillows
their kids in the garage. How he shaped

with his own skilled hands
his oldest son, landscaper extraordinaire, well-mannered

hunter of neighborhood girls,
molester of his sisters.

You remember the phone call.
When she told you her son dreamed of touching

your daughter. You steel yourself.
Carve out a room inside yourself where you wait.

Fingering words like sterile instruments.
Stroking their sharp edges.

Will you let me write about my love for my child

or will you answer, *no, you are a sentimental woman?*
Will you let me say she's as beautiful as a ruby-
throated hummingbird, and as fragile?
That even in adolescence, she's conjoined
to my heart like a Siamese twin,
so if hers throbs with thrill
or slows with sense, mine does, too?
That if hers beats fight-flight-fight-flight-fight-

flight, my pulse batters my breast,
my blood circling like a hawk,
till it finds the juicy core, then dives?
That I long to release the beak
of fear, to stop eating
myself alive?

Blue

Little boy. And the color of his sleep. Deep within the day. His horn silent in the shadows of the stacks. Hushed as the hue of evening. That silken wrap around the sky's broad shoulders. Its fragrance fragile. Like a hydrangea, full as a bosom, baring its bloom in a crystal vase. Unfastening one petal the shade of a last breath. Letting it fall to the floor. And there it is: tinge of gloom. Like the glaze on my son's contact lens, flicked, accidentally, down the drain. And his hint of lamentation. Then: the pipe wrenched open. Lens lifted out. Unscratched. Ready for the rinse. Tint of vision lost, then found.

Sightseeing

We drove through Yellowstone,
    winding through its burnt edges,
blackened trees on one side,
    lush hills on the other,
in the middle of June.
    The traffic was heavy,
engines burning up serenity
    like fire consumes aspen
and pine, exhaust casting
    its dark shadow onto the road.
We slowed to a stop
    beside a buffalo
lounging like a Lab
    within the short length
of my arm. They have rules
    in the park, and this proximity
broke one. I could've touched
    its mane, full as a huckleberry bush,
brown as the earth itself.
    I could've fingered
the sharp tips of its horns.
    And while my kids tried to enforce
the law from the back seat,
    my husband nervous at the wheel,
I did what anyone does
    when she looks into the eyes
of endurance, crosses the border
    beyond belief. I rolled down
my window, zoomed in close,
    and snapped the picture.

Labor Day

Soap foams like spume on waves
    sloshing toward shore. And the water
is warm as I wipe each dish and fork
    like the sea wipes its sand-caked brow.

Summer is over. My kids sit at the table,
    doing their homework. My husband
outside, his tractor chugging,
    whittles away his work,

cutting square after shrinking square
    into our lawn. Clouds crowd the blue
in the September sky, squeezing
    the sun into one long beam

leaning like a ladder against the air,
    stretching through my window.
I sense the cold feet
    of winter on the top rung,

heading down. But the water is warm
    as it spills from the spigot like light.
My hands clinging to the cup
    that now runs over.

Where the Rain Clears

Standing on the street
in the early morning of late autumn,

I marvel to see, to my left,
over my own backyard, rain

and to my right, over my neighbor's barn,
only clear, dry air.

As I walk this line
drawn by the ordinary length of asphalt,

I think of the theologian who said,
God is on the loose now,

no longer hidden behind
the parochet, waiting for the high priest

to ask for the atonement
of his people's sins.

The rain has to clear somewhere.
Why not here? Like the road has rent

a veil that cloaks the fullness
of sight, separates shade from light.

A Clear Path

He drives his red truck to the field,
the farmer who once ran into our mailbox, saying,
You people and your big houses git in the way.

This harvest day, from our window,
my son and I watch him and his pal stretch
tape measure from a fence post, then a road sign,

to our mailbox across the way. They nod at one another,
hop back into his Chevy. A good ol' boy telepathy.
Then he pulls into our drive, reverses in a straight line,

rams the gold-and-black sign, throwing caution
to the ground. We blink in disbelief as he grabs
a chainsaw from the back, rips

through the base of the post in five seconds flat.
And drives away,
kicking up our confusion with the gravel.

And I'm sad as I recall writing about the vulture
that once perched on that post. Both are gone now.
A clear path often means loss.

But within minutes, his combine emerges
like a realization, turns the corner, skirts
past my mailbox, lowers its enormous blade,

and plows into the grain like a tidal wave.

Eating Her Way through December

1.

My black Lab nabbed my son's Bible
like they say Christ will snatch His own.

True, she wasn't in a cloud, didn't shout or sound a trumpet.
She'd been outside. Cold air in her lungs

fueling her nerve, she raised her front paws
to the table, grabbed the book, and—I do not lie!—

devoured Ezekiel.
Gnawing especially on his confession

that when God told him, he ate His
Word, and it slid down his throat like honey.

2.

Maggie's been stealing ornaments from the tree.
Low ones that aren't breakable (I've learned to place them there)

like the old gingerbread star (she smelled
cinnamon) and the plastic photo bell.

I keep yelling at her, barking out a new command,
Bad tree! following my sister's advice,

attaching the word *bad*, like a sticker,
to whatever she isn't supposed to touch.

But how can she help herself? She's used to sniffing
every tree she meets and chasing leaves like mice.

And those hundreds of lights!
Don't they draw us all like pole to contrary pole?

She's just a dog, you say. *She has no such sense.*
Fair enough. But look at her now:

See the lamb she chomps on, ceramic lamb she's lifted
from the manger beneath the tree?

One December Evening

Violin strings in their long, deep river of song . . .

Deer, seven of them: their white breath
mingling with snow adrift in darkness
till it melts on their blood-warm backs
anointing their baritone bodies . . .

Here is Handel's chorus of hallelujahs.
Rise.

Buck

The wild has come to your door:
A buck with a rack elaborate as a labyrinth
curving into dead ends.
Approaching the road you drive on.
Considering, perhaps, the lilies of the field
across the way. Threatening
to bolt, hurl his heavy heart
onto your hood.

He stands there,
staring at you as you pass,
turning your head toward him
like he's called you by name,
a name you have long since forgotten
and can't believe he knows.

Planting a Tree

My husband planted a tree in the dog's yard.
The poor sapling didn't have a chance.

Held by its stake, it stood its ground through storms
and wicked winds pushing through the plains.

But there was no hope. Our Lab couldn't learn
how to unravel her line when she'd wrap

around that lean tree. She's all exuberance
at the sight of us. All charge and jump.

So the maple snapped,
leaving behind a stub like a corn stalk after the harvest.

John meant to pull it out, restore the soil.
But it stayed all winter.

Then May arrived in sundress and heels,
blossoms in her hair.

And shoots burst through the stump like fireworks,
exploding with green.

Stealth

Like a big, black boomerang
    thrown into the air some twenty miles away
        the Stealth flew over our heads
            as we stood in our yard, gawking
        and our neighbors zoomed in
    to photograph the slow and silent
majesty of man.

Someone proclaimed
    What a great country
        yet the plane seemed sustained
            not by some ingenious engineering
        but by steam: It was July
    and hot as firecrackers, the broad shoulders
of humidity holding strong.

The killdeer, unfazed
    ran its conspicuous mission
        Operation Fake Broken Wing
            squealing and scampering down the road
        to lure the cat, crouching
    in the grass, eyes locked
on its target, away from the nest.

And the cows weren't impressed
    as they bowed their heads
        to pull grass from the ground's
            loose grasp. They knew
        no difference in the pasture
    as the ticks climbed, unnoticed
up their fur-lined hides.

Kyrie Eleison

For thence,—a paradox
Which comforts while it mocks,—
Shall life succeed in that it seems to fail . . .

—Robert Browning

Mockingbirds flutter by, flashing
the white patches on their gray wings
amid their dance, flaunting before us
the way all lovers do with their public displays
of affection. We talk about whether we'll reach 50,
my husband and I, sitting on the front porch,
bemoaning the many ways our health
has failed. One mockingbird pulls
a refrain from his ever-expanding
repertoire. *Come*, he seems to croon.
Grow old along with me.
We long for the years of our young
marriage when we solved each ache
with Tylenol. One swallow. And done.
The other mockingbird, now perched on our roof,
chatters away, sending forth a tune
we cannot translate, a mystery that envelops us.
I look at my husband and love him more and more
and want to call to him like these birds,
want to tell him that we, too, may be a song
on some untamed tongue.

Remember Blessing

When you see blood run like hell
down car-bombed streets or smell the fire
of guns in your red-brick schools,
when you taste the metal
of unjust war or feel the fields
quake from the screams of children
fettered to the long arm
of a godless law,

when you blink,
hoping you will open your eyes
and all these pictures will have vanished
and the world is actually a good place,
but they don't, and it's not,
when you've lost your faith,

remember blessing.

You will already know sin
is real—how it sucks breath
from the lungs of joy—
and that sometimes, you are guilty.
You will already know pain.
And the evil that mushrooms
when power is at stake.

So remember then
the way you walked through your yard in the summers
of your youth, searching for the only treasure
within reach, a star glittering on the blushing
face of quartz, sun tapping stone
with its magic wand.

Remember the way the soil felt on your fingertips as you dug in.

Remember the ant toting its nugget toward its hill,
the grasshopper leaping
onto your lap, the worm's nose
rising into the air, as if to sniff your skin.

Remember your brother, or your sister, close by,
digging, too, the dirt's musky aroma,
your sweat, and the moment of discovery,
lifting the pink fingerprint
of God from the earth.

Window

Caught in the slim cell between pane and screen,
a robin, desperate to go out

the way it came in,
flapped its wings with fury.

It had flown into the web of wire,
ensnaring itself as it broke through,

hit glass. Though I lifted
the sash, the red breast

pushed forward, refusing
to turn around, fly into the garage,

out the raised door.
We feared its wing would tear

from its shoulder, that its heart
would melt from the instinct burning

behind the bars of its ribs.
So we unhinged the panel from the jamb,

like removing a gate from a cage,
releasing the bird into the morning air,

then followed it, stretching
our bodies through the window

that seemed, in the mercy
of the moment, to go on opening

and opening.